Words of Isolation

Abhra Pal

I am walking with you at every step, at every stumble, at every breath.
I am walking with you, at every turn.
At every crossroads
I am as baffled as you are.

To my father
who I know used to write secretly and would be happiest
man today if he lived see this book

About this book

April is a special month for poets. It is observed as national poetry writing month, in solidarity with American writers who coined the term. It is now more widely known as global poetry writing month, urging poets to write a poem every day of this month. I started writing this collection in the infamous 2020, when the world witnessed a rather unprecedented event that brought most of the moving parts of life to a standstill.

Writing poetry is an exhausting process as it is. Together with the newfound misfortune of virtual chains around our ankles along with financial and mental miseries, it put us in a sordid state of creative cripple. Certainly not an uplifting mood for writing. I have been writing poetry since I was very young but, if anything, I was never very frequent with it. I had my moments with poetry as well as a prolonged dry period of nothingness. As life took me from one place to another world, it also gave me a new depth to poetry. It was not until this fateful Melbourne autumn of 2020 that I brought myself to write a poem every day. It was full of agony, despair, and memories – through and through.

About this book

I have procrastinated the idea of publishing for a long time – under any other circumstance, I would never let them see the light of the day.

However, I let the manuscript age instead, allowing the raw emotions to settle. I did not throw it away because it was an ambitious project, even though it wasn't ready. When all the restrictions started, I could not come to accept the isolation, like many others. Everyday news was succumbing to the darkness around. Back home in India, millions were left at mercy of fate, as they travelled thousands of miles across the country. I lost my father just before Covid hit this world and it was not easy for me to accept his sudden passing. I found his memories made their way into my writing. Undeniably, my sadness became the centrepiece for this collection. After I let the writing age, it started evolving into what it is now. I borrowed some of the words I wrote previously but left them unfinished in my notebooks. I often saw darkness as the death of desire and romance, but as the four walls became my new normal, I found new heart-warming tales of romance, which balanced the plethora of gloom I had already poured myself into. Today we are opening up about mental health awareness like never before. I feel I have seen the worst up close. I do not know how much of it transpired into my writing. I hope the aspiration of freedom, the spirit to live in spite of all the darkness, prevails.

Today, I have decided to let them see the light of the world. In the darkness, a spirit of light and self-discovery.

Abhra Kumar Pal

Words of Isolation

Chapter 1

Cherish

The winter morning seeps into
the balminess of my blanket,
warm tea on my lips
and the comfort of my armchair.

Love or hate, spirals face downwards
they caught me unguarded
left my troubled soul
thirsting for more.

Today is humble
compared to the lively past,
I harbour my roving ship to little joys,
and keep fears at bay.

The untamed ocean at my feet
swaying, reminding
there is no soulmate
waiting at the end of the world.

Abhra Pal

Come evening, many hearts
will eloquently chirp as birds
we are alone, but for once
we can cherish the water of loneliness.

Chapter 2

Present

*Your past is not my past,
and my memories
are not yours.*

*Dip your pen
in my joy
and you would have a vibrant canvas.*

*Dip your tongue
in my sorrow
and it would leave an insipid taste.*

*We live the life of a river,
failure of a rock,
and waves of expectations.*

*Yet our present
is an infinite chance
at happiness.*

Abhra Pal

*All of us
die a little
everyday.*

*Love has us build a boat
our will is an oar,
we sail across paper oceans.*

Chapter 3

Afterlife

I

*The birds
on my grave
will sing
in
casual
cacophony.*

*Returning
to the shade
at the end
of the day,
hungry,
thirsty
and numb-winged.*

Little

would they know,
I took
the seed
of a great tree
to the grave
for them.

They must not,
for every grave
on earth
should
turn
to a tree
in the afterlife.

After death
I became
a wizard of sorts.

Suddenly
I was
omnipresent.

Navigating
the crossroads
of past and future.

Words of Isolation

*I went to pet
the German Shepherd
I had growing up.*

*I witnessed
my grandchild
take her first steps.*

*I found a myriad of colours
in morning light dispersed from my
    window pane
like never before.*

*Darkness
revealed
its secrets to me.*

*The unknown
was not a
mystery anymore.*

*A moment does not go by
when my children do not
think of me.*

*I told them
I am never really gone,
and they could all agree for once.*

*After death
everything
became easier.*

Chapter 4

Unnamed colour

We will continue to talk poetry
so long as there is
mystery in it

Describing a thought
without naming
makes the poets who they are

Not words, rhymes or metres
not meaning, memory or quest
we bathe in colours

Living, breathing,
aching, screaming
larger than life

If death descends
on my eyelids
let it be swift

Words of Isolation

I am tired of
fighting battles
that are not mine

Spare me the vanity:
I intuit
broken all around me

Till the very end,
tuck me in
the colour of trust

Sing to me
a book of love
retold a thousand lives before

Remind me with your eyes,
we are never too dead
to live again.

Chapter 5

Element

*Does it surprise you
that most of our stories
have a memorable beginning
but not an end?*

*I have had my share
of perpetual fear,
now I give it a name,
put it in a box.*

*A mirror
hangs on the wall
reflecting
an unwelcome reminder.*

*Your eyes get numb too,
you hide behind them
smear your looks,
wash your walls with tears.*

Words of Isolation

*Love lives its age,
as we live ours
it is not the only element
life stands upon.*

*Let us lean
on compassion,
but drink to the pain
that made us more resilient than yesterday.*

Chapter 6

Plight

*This too, shall pass
I will scribble
my way out of this.*

*I will leisurely
succumb to gluttony,
and walk out of this.*

*I will headhunt spite
and jibber jabber
out of this.*

*I will infuse blood with cringe
and stockpile
out of this.*

*This too shall pass
so long as the proletariat,
continues to carry our finesse on their strong
    shoulders.*

Words of Isolation

Life has figured out our constraints,
has us huddled within walls
matchboxes, squabbling before a spark
    eats us.

Fear has laid us bare,
put our ugly faces on
yet we harbinger illusion of safety, security
    and sanity.

This too, shall pass
we will hope
our way out of this.

Chapter 7

Progeny

I

*It started on a Sunday
when I found
your journal, while
cleaning out an old closet.*

*The art of words
magic of
curved letters,
ink fading on tarnished pages.*

*It started on a Sunday
when I succumbed
to the incessant
charm of wordplay.*

*Now they suddenly surface
on a frosty mirror
or gloomy clouds*

Words of Isolation

waving by captive afternoon.

You did not let me look down,
today you fill me
with a lungful of air
when I wear out.
The glory of you
is the glory of me,
a burden
I must write on.

2

Dad used to tell me: the ocean may take a lot
but never keeps anything for itself
returns everything it takes

He said, and I believed
like a lot of other things
he said

Saw all the shells and rocks
at my feet, and wondered
where were they taken from

I live inside an ocean today
gushing enormous depth around me
every day, something gets taken

I cry, I scream
none of that comes back

leaving me alone, except for cold licks

Dad probably wasn't fully right, no one
    truly is
but he saw things come back
just not exactly where they were taken

We cry, we scream
just because sometimes
we do not know where to look

All of us live in an ocean
hopes we give up
will eventually come back.

Chapter 8

Home

*You know, in my mind palace
I've now built a glass house
glass flooring, walls and ceiling
where we see and feel everything*

*Garden grass seeds shooting up
from its warm & moist earthy bed,
a world of vanity across glass walls
wrapping the naked and truest us*

*The sky above, unashamed, emotional
from racing clouds to dancing rain
we see it all, we brace it all and then
the starry jewels descend upon us*

*A glass house, you see, holds the
forbidden destiny we're sailing for
it takes time, it takes tides to ride
A clandestine opaque glass house*

Abhra Pal

I adorn you with flowers in your ears
Jewels around neck, waist and
anklets tinkling as you softly walk
with my words all over you, love

A future worth sailing on — a home
for our unnamed, untamed love
Leaving behind a lifetime of brooding
Walk with me tonight, will you, my dove?

Chapter 9

Journey

*The long-distance train
slowly took off, munching its wheels
whistles shrilled through.*

*A typical thick smell of people, street foods
    and smoke
started fading, but the
salt of your lips was still wet on mine.*

*Tears I was holding on to
until everything
faded around me.*

*Little did I know
strangers could cry so comfortably
in front of each other's deceitful smile.*

*I sobbed
every passing second*

*sultry with the copious amount of your
    embrace.*

*I broke
unlucky in love,
and came out as a changed man.*

*All it took
was a fateful journey,
the train is still munching, whistling, all the
    same.*

Chapter 10

Carpe Diem

*Standing in front of a massive door
I wait and you don't even know
I've arrived.*

*If only you'd open the door
we would fly away
Yet we wait for someone else to open it.*

*Unlike a book,
open and you've got to read it
the book, once opened, desires to read.*

*Those words, black ink
pages housing emotions,
lures you in.*

*We both know,
I'm not talking about books
You are my book, home to my fervour.*

Chapter 11

Unsaid

I see you, across the road, waiting for me. I wave at you. A smile shines on your lips. The dullness of my afternoon wanes from little joys blossoming in our hearts. It has been quite a wait. We know. We know all sorts of unknowns about each other.

I do not run, or leap forward. I wait for the traffic. Savouring this moment seems to be more important than running to you. A hug, a melting embrace, melting of distance and wait absorbis traces of want. Breath-disappearing words, play softly in my head as I walk.

You know all this. It's no secret, this is ours. I walk slower than the passing clouds.

Your arms wait for me.

"Where do you want to go?" you ask me.
"Nowhere but here" I smile.

Then we walk. I tell you about my week and

you tell me about your decade. We omit chapters, characters from our stories inadvertently. The world moves very fast around us. Tectonic plates collide. I try to helplessly capture a moment. You smile,

"Did you just almost ruin our near perfect moment by taking a picture?"

"Did I now?" I ask.

Sun gets numb. Wind gets stronger. The quiet turns into rustles.

The last leaf of the season falls from a tree. I look into your eyes. We do not have eternity. We do not have happily ever after. We have this. I take your hand firmly. Even after the grasp, the tips of my fingers caress the long wait awaiting us.

We can ink the moment with a kiss, or maybe we don't have to.

Chapter 12

Eloquent

How are your eyes today?
Calm before the storm
Or numb after the rain?

The more mysteries you hide
the more eloquent they become
I know your eyes all too well

In silence, they storm
In dreams, they paint
You won't believe the treasures you hide.

The maddening outcry
often swallows itself,
weakness becomes prison

Everything once cherished
now deserted
don't condemn yourself unloved

Words of Isolation

we have confided our keys to one another,
what has separated us, ironically
is also what connected us.

How are your eyes today?
Calm before the storm
Or numb after the rain?

Chapter 13

Language of flowers

*Choose silence
and flowers
will speak for you.*

*Don't open up to each other;
the flowers in your bouquet
will give away the warm feelings*

*Our emotions
don't hide so well
behind petals*

*We have given them shades
friendship, peace, love
and let the flowers speak passion*

*then there'll be time to go
all of a sudden
sadly, silently,*

Words of Isolation

*Do not leave a white wreath
adorn me with the reddest rose,
when I am gone.*

*At peace, finally
I might be, but I choose
to be more alive than ever.*

Chapter 14

Bridge

*A firm hold isn't just a firm hold
You and I - we built a bridge a long time ago,
without knowing.*

*You gave me a taste of mysteries
I gave you
delicious shame from sudden freedom.*

*Unclasping you in your blouse,
turning those lips red
for me to drink.*

*A firm hold isn't just a firm hold
It's trust, care and strength
yielded in warmth.*

*We found pleasure of unknowns
at twenty, till misfortune
suddenly walked in.*

Words of Isolation

*Your hair
swayed like a rope bridge,
between two hills.*

*I kept talking
you cosied in my firm grips,
I wanted the storm of your eyes.*

*A firm hold isn't just a firm hold
It's need, lust and desire
forged in a shield.*

*You nudged me to stop
yet danced, so that I would not
Our bridge, swaying, forever.*

Chapter 15

Steal

In my right mind,
I can never claim
I did not steal anything.

I plagiarised colours
from the sunsets and forests
into my palette.

I danced in the pure joy
of children
running to candy and ice creams.

I borrowed patience
from the silence
of the oldest trees.

I stole time
when I caught you
looking at me.

Words of Isolation

I stole fortitude
from the bed of rocks
as I bled but walked on.

Your scent
grew on me
as your love made me bloom, one petal a day.

In our right mind,
We can never possibly claim
We didn't steal one another.

Chapter 16

Inspirations

*You could have had a wide forest
but you chose to plant
a tiny seed,
in my heart.*

*You never set foot on the affluence of comfort
but you helped me
befriend pain
at a tender age.*

*I walked on and on
discovering
my world with
disillusion.*

*Sinking into quicksand of troubles
I saw the roots
from the tiny seed
you planted, and I clasped it for dear life.*

Words of Isolation

You left a lot unsaid
and now I have found my voice
your dreams and my dictions,
I feel will surely meet somewhere.

Chapter 17

Gullible

*I keep staying up late
at my desk,
with the dim light on*

*Rest of the night
gone to rest
silently*

*My stomach,
content with a lovely dinner and the
warmth of snug fabric on my skin*

*somewhere out there
away from my
sweet home*

*there are people
in agony, in frustration, in loneliness, in pain
painting this time red*

Words of Isolation

who will live to tell?
a tale
so uncertain

Storytellers are tiptoeing
a thin balance,
something they do so well
conceal which side they are on

we don't know
if closure
is on the horizon

we are merely in luck,
that we are born
and alive with poetry.

Chapter 18

Forgotten

*Those yellow, crisp pages
of my old journal I left unsaid,
weighing one insignificant memory over
    another
speaks volumes.*

*Getting older, wearier
did not have enough of
the first, cheap fountain pen
that taught me to flow like a stream*

*As days go by
fingers, more dutiful to plastic keys,
make us wear
the unreal world
like a second skin*

*I watch the clouds sway
river waves chuckle,
swoon over seasons shedding colours*

Words of Isolation

feel the wet dew drops on bare feet
often left mesmerized
by the unsaid.

We are building memoirs,
in our own ways
forgetting
simple joys,
or, what they ever were.

Chapter 19

Pleasures

*Morning walks in with
strong caffeine between our lips
sun dancing at our bare feet, off the blanket
for three and half minutes more*

*Eyes numb from the
sleep deprived passion
soaking in every bit of stimuli
healing, breathing*

*Some laughter
some soliloquy
some banter
pillow talks resonating, restoring, nourishing*

*It matters little
whether you wake me up or I you,
so long as we brace the morning
and not sneak out*

Words of Isolation

Wearing our true scents
with morning mist,
word games played
with fingertips.

We are both good at one thing
mischievously corrupting
the other, as every part of me
mates with each part of you.

Morning is about to leave
reminding us:
the aftermath of intimacy
is only the beginning.

Chapter 20

Healer

*I have had a long walk
since I set out for life
and aged with
valleys, deserts and plateaus*

*Every time I came
across a stone
brilliantly hued or not
I picked it up and placed it in my sack*

*I grew older as
my sack started getting heavier
difficult to carry
all the stones all the time*

*One day, fatigued, I stopped
next to a river
dipped my numb and sore feet
into the cold current*

Words of Isolation

And what did I see?
The riverbed was laced with an
array of gorgeous pebbles
each shinier than the other

Tears that spurted
became a river,
what didn't
turned into a stone

It was the day
I chose to let go of my sovereigns
became the healer
I was destined to be.

Chapter 21

Mixtape

*We believed
friendship could
stand the test of time
we couldn't be more wrong.*

*We naively
gave into the idea
we could be timeless
and reality eluded us.*

*We hummed
our favourite rock music
all put in a mixtape,
magnetic memories on a magnetic film.*

*Facades fell before us
races, families, languages
never posed a
barrier.*

Words of Isolation

*We were go-getters
treasured knick-knacks
sulked sometimes, or laughed at our failures
time wrote, some of us, off.*

*The old mixtape
still sings to us
as young as
memories will forever be.*

Chapter 22

Fallen

*We mourn as the new stars surface
on the darkest of nights, and
petals fall silently
from our precious flowers*

*The burden of spirits is heavy
enough to make us sink
into guilt and fear
that lives beneath our skin*

*As some wait forever,
some roads have no return
some goodbyes are so interlaced
with unworldly love*

*I have had a taste of the fate
and my father before me,
we are not merely who we are
years of fallen stand behind us.*

Chapter 23

Llover a cántaros

Prelude:

Literal translation: to rain to pitchers
English meaning: to rain cats and dogs

1

The city,
numb & fatigued,
weeks of torment
from ruthless heat
Cried silently, 'paint me green'
and the sky
so vehemently endowed
Us, poets,
sentenced to the
captivity of windows

2

Abhra Pal

When there is a reason
to fly back
in time, it just happens
A time when we used
to write letters,
gift wrapped love, in words
One of those days
when I took
my joy to rain
One of those days
hopelessly loved
Awash with intimate rain

3

Dear Poet,
it's cold outside
Melbourne's raining

Dear Poet,
the colours are
blending, flourishing

Dear Poet,
subtle greens of suburbs
becoming verdant

Dear Poet,
sadness will eat you
if you don't let it out

4

Words of Isolation

The world is getting dry,
rain to pitchers
let us see our tears washed
Running straight into peril
that's so us
that's our selfish, mortal dream
Our destiny is boxed
into materials & coloured dreams
can we watch them wash away?
We don't see death
until we hit it
though we ride a harrowing life
Outdid our own ambitions
with selfish dryness
Can we watch them, washed over?

Chapter 24

The love fruit

*It is hard to decide
if the mangoes
I grew up with
were sweeter
than the childhood*

*Memories of taste
eavesdropped
into silent afternoons
of tropical summers.*

*Before they ripened
to near round
mouth-watering
deliciousness.*

*They did shower
taste buds with
raw, sour, shivering
tanginess.*

Words of Isolation

*My coming-of-age stories
often intertwine with mangoes
a perfect semblance
of tastes at war.*

*I will let you in a secret
the mango crush
goes incredibly well
with vodka shots.*

Chapter 25
Almanac

*Fate of a fortune
words of wisdom
whispering in thin air
of celestial signs*

*Every year
comes the wishy-washy
with juxtaposition
of life and loss.*

*Today, when everything
is in question,
every belief
belittles fate.*

*We have fallacies at hand
we have our share of misfortune
crops drying
lives slowly rolling to their death.*

Words of Isolation

*Fate of a fortune
unknown mysteries
our make-believe future
is only as weak as our strongest fear.*

Chapter 26

Muse

*We are often blinded by our eyes
we see only what eyes can see
we see dreams the way
we are conditioned to.*

*'Lend me your voice'
she whispered to the waves,
sand mesmerised her skin
she wore the perfect wild scent*

*Poised with moist wind, she coiled
her urges had her saturated,
as salt did the ocean
she was both fire and water*

*the simplest girl for the world
she wore a map to lost hearts of men
unpretentious flow meandering
across many fertile minds*

Words of Isolation

*Her fleeting looks into our eyes
led us to the taverns of oldest desire
her demure walk resonated with hearts
as we all swooned over her*

*Her eyes read us inside out
she was not here to make us fall in love
she was a river of love,
since the beginning of lust.*

Chapter 27

Room on the roof

*So much is trapped in there
between cobwebs and
thick wooden varnish
- a room on the roof.*

*Sweaty summers and monsoon dances
curious nights of chasing dreams
or stargazing for a nearing planet.*

*It was a perfect home
for paintings, journals
and everything unfinished
ideas born, ideals followed.*

*Adolescents painted
sultry kisses and fear
while a noisy table fan rustled
and a rugged bed squirreled.*

A room where nothing happens

Words of Isolation

*no comfort or luxury will ever come of it,
except for the space one needs.*

*We are building a new world order
who would build
a room on the roof anymore?*

Some will preserve them, though.

Chapter 28

Sacred lust of your name

We love mysteries
Moth to fire,
drawn towards what we won't understand;
Exploring a young, untamed river
With a tiny hope-boat
& strong oar of will.

I met you, in a state of perdition
a melee of emotions
shameless
to claim your pristine
But you, lit a lamp, patiently
At peace with my unrest
and my boat found an anchor

We are yet to anticipate
You and I
Can be the
long winding road
Short of eternity as we know it

Words of Isolation

*Yet, sailing together, boat swaying
amid current, rains
& turbulent sea*

*You may be quiet in the morning
and yet I ache for you
You may be busy during the day
and yet I burn for you
You may be at peace in the evening
and yet I shiver for you
our poise is a balance*

*I want us to find
pleasure that is the forgotten
truth of civilization,
live out the trifles of
of this materialistic world,
drink tears that fill the void
with smoke from the incense of our spirits*

*Sacred lust of your name
is my fragrance,
As mine is yours
I know our boat will sail
Till we become the ocean
Ourselves*

Chapter 29

Motley

I

I remember the day when we met
it was such
an unceremonious occasion

our
shy hands
took to weakest fingers

and forged
something stronger and bigger
than both of us

one
joyful step
of togetherness

paved
the path of

Words of Isolation

thousand unknowns

2

*You come to my balcony often
and look at the horizon*

*Look at Mount Macedon ranges
and the everlasting clouds*

*Your quiet and coy smile shines,
as the wine swirls in a fine glass*

*my touch and whispers
about to play magic*

you are my harp

3

*I say the same thing
every time
we make love*

*you squirm delightfully
tiptoeing
the line of*

Abhra Pal

yes and maybe

I say the same thing
every time
you brace it

senses are reborn

4

what if I was made for you
and you
did not know
how to read?

we wear
such ancient symbols,
lost in obscure spots

It takes
a miracle of touch
for the pores to open

I wait for you
and you for me
unaware how long we have been destined

to reach
each

into
other's deep

5

The walls are falling
lines are getting blurred

it is a fun moment
to decide
who takes over in this game
neither is afraid of losing

those dangerously
slippery slopes
that define

the utopia of climax
or the next beginning

6

After the storm
if we
bag our fear

Abhra Pal

and step out

another
storm
would still wait
across some horizon

I was
only worried
for a safe forever
yet I forgot

today
isn't about
anything else
but today

The stars inked on your neck
unabashedly dare me
to move past them

as if you do not have
enough ammunition already
to make me fall

the curled soft lips
is an inescapable trap

Words of Isolation

yet you bare
your freshly inked neck

I look into your eyes
you plummet
into my kiss

trust we bought
with a free fall

8

There is no denying
the aching tension
is unbearable

The air of unfulfilled ambitions
strings us
together

Us, here, now
entangle with the
quasi-constant eternity

we will devour each other
there is no running away
from it

9

You reckon
this titillating swordplay
is a battle?

whether the wave
gets stopped by the rock
or the rock
gets lashed by untamed waves

they are
equally fateful
I see them as one

Ironic
how we love and hate
the same thing

a storm
cold and cruel
can still celebrate lovers

10

The golden of your skin
against the

Words of Isolation

scarlet of sunset

as light
transcends
last eight minutes of
its penultimate flight
of the day from sun

the molten lava
of that golden passion
dribbles through
my intestine

a golden last kiss
for eight breathless minutes

11

I take your hand
and you guide me
from one heaven
to another

no fine satin
no earthly bed
can write
such joyous vibes
to our pleasure's pores,
I'll tell you that

12

*When I look
into those delicate
innocent
eyes of yours
twinkling*

*When I take
a moment
to let those lush lips
swell, a bit more
after merciless
subjugation
and compare with
the unceremonious dame*

*I remind myself
how important it is
to look beneath the shell*

13

*Look in the mirror
you will see*

Words of Isolation

two broken people

Look at the stars above
you will see
a version of completeness

We tell our hearts
stories
harmless enough
to live by

Tear down those walls &
Look into each other

you will see
serendipity

Write off those thin
subtle marks
from oozing passion,
will you?

pleasure
is not the centre
of everything
but it's what makes
our moment

Abhra Pal

*ignore not
for the abyss
isn't short lived*

*Darkness
even your own
has good and bad written over it*

*Let's say
you
turned away*

*It'd be hard
to believe
you're shy*

*you face away from
the territories
unexplored*

*you face away
but don't
hide
those
very vocal
pleasure strings
your back*

Words of Isolation

my hands

your canvas
my brushes
we paint
till inks run out

We write our story
as two
intertwined
thirsty
ill-fated
strangers

think
of the barriers
we have overcome
thus far

our subtle
art of artlessness
is truly sublime.

*We define
what we want
this moment
to be
the vines
that we embody
in our embrace*

*the nectar
we suck*

*the elixir
of our purest*

*the shadows we cast
to the mysteries
of past*

*the sunshine
we glow
into each other*

*today
we bloom*

Words of Isolation

*I have been
searching
for you,
in you
that one tiny spot
of purity*

*One
that is synonymous
with your soul
and not so humble
cry for irresistible
unending
crescent*

*pleasure dwindles
right there
a far cry
a deep
search*

*lovers swim a lifetime
in the quest*

About the Author

Abhra Pal was born in a small town near Kolkata, India. He was schooled at the Ramakrishna Mission and went on to attain a degree in Electronics and Communication. He now lives in Melbourne, Australia, where he works full time in IT as a Senior Solution Architect in Financial Services.

As a creative at heart, Abhra has always enjoyed writing and poetry was among his first loves. He has dabbled in it for many years, submitting many items of work to poetry magazines but now has finally put together his own collection of poems for an even wider audience.

Written over poetry writing month, when the Covid pandemic was threatening the world, Abhra created an individual verse for every day of the month that centre on memories, love and life, and is certain to offer readers something of a glimpse of their own lives.

Today, Abhra enjoys his new life in Australia and in his free time enjoys spending lots of it with his young daughter, who has inherited his own creative streak. He also enjoys photography, creative writing in both English and Bengali, watching films and making some of his own as well.

As someone who has travelled widely in his life, including most of India and the UK, Abhra is keen to see other parts of the world that he has not yet found his way to. He is also keen to publish a novel one day, while continuing to pen beautiful poetry that readers can relate to.

You can contact Abhra Pal at:
Email: abhra.pal@gmail.com

www.ingramcontent.com/pod-product-compliance
Lightning Source LLC
Chambersburg PA
CBHW020329010526
44107CB00054B/2039